Tricks in Swift

By Julien FAUJANET

Table of contents

Table of contents

Introduction

In this book we will see some tips and interesting algorithms to simplify life in Swift language, for programming on IOS. The version of Swift used here is 3.0.

This book is for Swift programmers who have the basics of language and want to know tricks and / or shortcuts, rather than looking for several hours on the forums.

In the first chapter we will see how to post on social networks Facebook and Twitter (and even with Image).

In the next chapter we will learn to retrieve a photo from the IPhone gallery (or Ipad).

Then we will manage the Collections (by creating a scrolling system as on the applications of Filters)

In the next chapter we will talk about Layers, which will allow us to manage the rendering of our elements like for example: to make round the edges of a button.

After that we will attack the Extensions which is a very interesting feature that will allow us to modify (in some ways) the behavior of the component classes in Swift.

Then we'll see how to convert a View to UIImage.

Next chapter: It will be the ScrollView that will be addressed, to move on content that is larger than the screen of your device and manage the zoom.

The alerts that we will see later, are in fact dialog boxes. But they will be very useful to you.

Post on social networks

We will start by seeing how to publish on Facebook. The method we will use here is very simple. We need to import the "Social" module to use it.
Like this :

```
8
9    import UIKit
10   import Social
11
```

Import Social module

Now create a button that will be used to start sharing on Facebook and in the function that runs when you press the button insert the following code:

```
if SLComposeViewController.isAvailable(forServiceType: SLServiceTypeFacebook){
    var facebookSheet:SLComposeViewController = SLComposeViewController(
        forServiceType: SLServiceTypeFacebook)

    self.present(facebookSheet, animated: true, completion: nil)
} else {
    var alert = UIAlertController(
        title: "Accounts",
        message: "Please login to a Facebook account to share.",
        preferredStyle: UIAlertControllerStyle.alert)

    alert.addAction(UIAlertAction(
        title: "OK",
        style: UIAlertActionStyle.default,
        handler: nil))

    self.present(alert,
                animated: true,
                completion: nil)
}
```

The code of the function to share a post on Facebook

To sum it up, this code tests if the Facebook service is available and displays the sharing window if it is the case, otherwise the window which will be displayed will ask you to enter your identifiers.

You can compile your code and try it by pressing the button. You should see a modal window appear as on the following capture:

Facebook post that we are about to publish

Enter your text and your post settings and press Publish.

Go take a look at Facebook to see the fruit of your (short) work. You should find a Post similar to the one of the following capture (obviously, the name of the person who posted this status will be different since it will be your Facebook account)

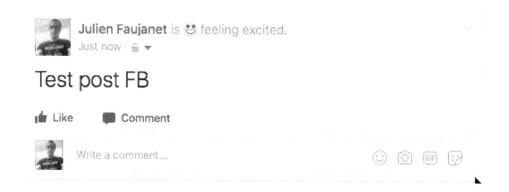

A Facebook post created and published in Swift language

Now let's see how to share an image in the status.

To share an image in a Facebook status the function is the same but you will have to add a line in the code. It is enough to inform which image one wishes to attach to the post by using the add method of our facebookSheet object.

Here is the line in question in the following capture:

```
facebookSheet.add(UIImage(named: "ColorCyanMonochrome.jpg")!)
```

The add method expects an object of type UIImage as argument. What I send him and my UIImage contains the name of the image I want to load.

As you can see, there is nothing simpler. I put you the complete code of the function on the following capture:

```
if SLComposeViewController.isAvailable(forServiceType: SLServiceTypeFacebook){
    var facebookSheet:SLComposeViewController = SLComposeViewController(
        forServiceType: SLServiceTypeFacebook)

    facebookSheet.add(UIImage(named: "ColorCyanMonochrome.jpg")!)
    self.present(
        facebookSheet,
        animated: true,
        completion: nil)
} else {
    var alert = UIAlertController(
        title: "Accounts",
        message: "Please login to a Facebook account to share.",
        preferredStyle: UIAlertControllerStyle.alert)

    alert.addAction(UIAlertAction(
        title: "OK",
        style: UIAlertActionStyle.default,
        handler: nil))

    self.present(
        alert,
        animated: true,
        completion: nil)
}
```

The code of the function that allows to publish a Facebook status with an image

I went to the line for more clarity on the screenshot, but the code is quite simple so it should not disturb you.

Here is the process when doing a test:

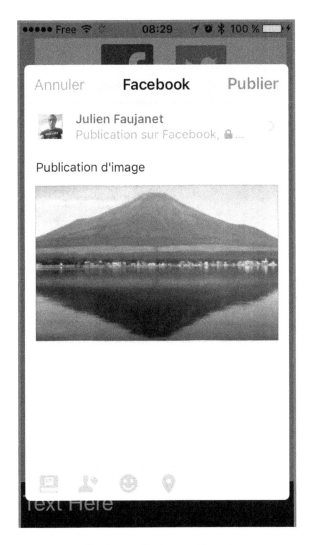

The image that we will post

You can of course edit anything you want, as if you were doing it from Facebook, such as: The audience setting, tagging one or more friends, or adding a mood status with the smiley that goes with it.

This is an image so this time the loading is longer, but when it is finished you will see the following screen:

The image is well published with the status

Here you now know how to publish on Facebook (Result on the next capture).

When you have assimilated this principle you will see that it is substantially the same thing to post a Tweet and this is also what we will see in the next paragraph.

Publication d'image

👍 Like   💬 Comment

 Write a comment...

Our post published with our picture

Post on Twitter

To post on Twitter the maneuver is the same. We still need the Social module. As for the code, here it is:

```swift
if SLComposeViewController.isAvailable(forServiceType: SLServiceTypeTwitter){
    var twitterSheet:SLComposeViewController = SLComposeViewController(
        forServiceType: SLServiceTypeTwitter)
    twitterSheet.setInitialText("Share on Twitter")

    self.present(
        twitterSheet,
        animated: true,
        completion: nil)
} else {
    var alert = UIAlertController(
        title: "Accounts",
        message: "Please login to a Twitter account to share.",
        preferredStyle: UIAlertControllerStyle.alert)

    alert.addAction(UIAlertAction(
        title: "OK",
        style: UIAlertActionStyle.default,
        handler: nil))

    self.present(alert, animated: true, completion: nil)
}
```

Code to publish a Tweet

You must put this code in a function that will run in support of your Twitter share button.

You may have noticed but there is a difference (two in fact). This is the setInitialText method that allows you to set a default text before sharing. I admit that this method also exists for Facebook but it does not work (which is probably due to a level of protection from Facebook).

As for the second (but that's logical) This is the type of service. We therefore replace here: SLServiceTypeFacebook by SLServiceTypeTwitter.

Let's try it. Launch your code and press your Twitter share button. You will see a modal window similar to the following:

Window to post a Tweet

Here is your window to post a Tweet (Warning: 140 characters ;-). Let's see the result on Twitter (see the following screenshot):

Julien FAUJANET @JulienFAUJANET · 3 s
Share on Twitter

Our freshly posted Tweet

And finally, let's see how to post an image on Twitter.

Post an image on Twitter

Here is the line to add in the code:

```
twitterSheet.add(UIImage(named: "ColorCyanMonochrome.jpg")!)
```

We add the image

As well as the complete code:

```
if SLComposeViewController.isAvailable(forServiceType: SLServiceTypeTwitter){
    var twitterSheet:SLComposeViewController = SLComposeViewController(
        forServiceType: SLServiceTypeTwitter)
    twitterSheet.setInitialText("Share on Twitter")
    twitterSheet.add(UIImage(named: "ColorCyanMonochrome.jpg")!)
    self.present(
        twitterSheet,
        animated: true,
        completion: nil)
} else {
    var alert = UIAlertController(
        title: "Accounts",
        message: "Please login to a Twitter account to share.",
        preferredStyle: UIAlertControllerStyle.alert)

    alert.addAction(UIAlertAction(
        title: "OK",
        style: UIAlertActionStyle.default,
        handler: nil))

    self.present(alert, animated: true, completion: nil)
}
```

Code for Tweet an image

I do not comment, it is almost identical to that of Facebook. Let's do a try instead:

Tweet an image

Result on the next capture. This chapter is now complete. So you know how to publish on Facebook and Twitter networks and even with images. In the next chapter we will see how to recover an image in the gallery of your device.

Julien FAUJANET @JulienFAUJANET · 7 s
Share on Twitter

Tweet with image from an IOS application

UIImagePicker

We will learn here to recover an image from the gallery of our device. For that we need to add the delegate of the UIImagePickerController at the top of our class as on the following capture:

```
class ViewController: UIViewController,UIImagePickerControllerDelegate,U
```

Our ViewController will have access to methods to manage Image Picker

Add a UIImageView to your ViewController to display the image when we retrieve it. Then eventually a button to trigger the opening of the image gallery (for my part, I will trigger this event to support the UIImageView, but do as you want).

In the function that will trigger the opening of the gallery insert the code of the next capture (I prefer to insert everything in a function to reuse it as I see fit when I want it, here it is):

```
func PickerLeftToSendInFunc(){
    let imagePicker = UIImagePickerController()   //notre controller.
    imagePicker.delegate = self    //le delegate pour recup la photo dans l'app.

    imagePicker.allowsEditing = false
    imagePicker.sourceType = .photoLibrary

    present(imagePicker,
            animated: true,
            completion: nil)
}
```

The code that will trigger the Controller

To make it simple we set our PickerViewController here and we call its function. Then insert the Controller function (see next screenshot) do not change its name:

```
// PickerController
func imagePickerController(_ imagePicker: UIImagePickerController,
                           didFinishPickingMediaWithInfo info: [String : AnyObject])
{
    var myImage = info[UIImagePickerControllerOriginalImage] as! UIImage
    ImageView_.image = myImage

    imagePicker.dismiss(animated: true, completion: nil)

}
```

The function of the PickerController

In this function we retrieve our image (when we have selected it in the phone gallery, or the tablet) and we store it in a variable (here: myImage), then we send this image in the image of our UIImageView (to display it on the screen) Here my UIImageView I named it ImageView_ but you can do it as you wish.

After that I use the dismiss method of the Picker because I do not need it anymore.

The last function we have to write is the one that will be launched if we cancel the selection of an image. This function is here:

```
//What to do if the image picker cancels.
func imagePickerControllerDidCancel(picker: UIImagePickerController) {
    picker.dismiss(animated: true, completion: nil)
}
```

The function that is started if the user cancels

A very important thing to do is to set your application to ask permission for the user to access the photo gallery of the device, otherwise it will not work (obviously it will be necessary for the user to accept for further).

Here's how to do it:

Go to your "info.plist" file and add the following line:

Privacy - Photo Library Usage Des... ⌄   String   Photo Library Needed

Do not forget to ask for access

The sentence on the left is truncated on the capture but with auto-completion you will see that the word that is cut is "Description".

Let's try it:

Click on the button that allows you to launch the PickerController, you will see the following modal window:

The application requests permission to access photos

You have to click OK to go further. We continue :

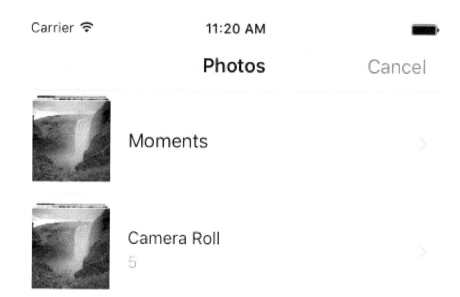

Photos Cancel

Moments ›

Camera Roll ›
5

We are in the photo gallery

I choose the album, then:

Point Reyes National Seashore
Mar 13, 2011 · Point Reyes Station, CA

Þingeyjarsveit, Northeast Iceland
Aug 8, 2012 · Goðafossvegur

Djúpavogshreppur
Aug 8, 2012 · East Iceland

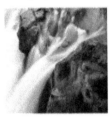

Rangárþing eystra
Aug 8, 2012 · South Iceland

Now I choose the photo I want to import into my application

Once I chose my photo:

The photo I chose

Here is my picture that appears in my UIImageView. I could of course choose "Cancel" instead of choosing the photo and it would not have been imported.

This chapter is now complete. You now know how to import a photo from your device gallery to display in your app. Do not forget to fill in the necessary permissions otherwise your code will not work.

UICollectionView

Here we will use the UICollectionView to manage element grids. But where it becomes interesting is that we will add the elements dynamically in the code, so that our grid adapts according to the number of elements it contains.

I specify that the elements we will manage are a collection of images where each of them will have a title. But I warn you, since the type of data we use in this chapter does not matter much, I will only use one image that will show up several times (I only had one). one on hand so we will do with).

As for the titles either, I did not break my head. I have named them: Title 1, Title 2, Title 3 etc. ... In short, let's start without further delay.

In your ViewController, add an item of type: CollectionView by dragging it:

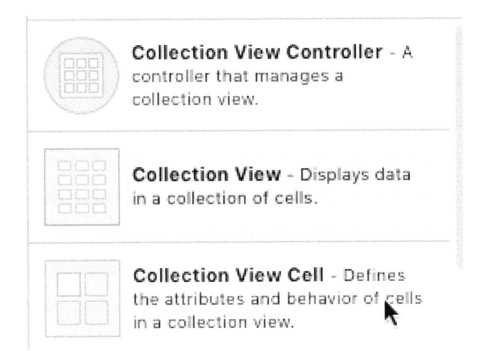

The CollectionView

Then make the CollectionView take the full width and height of your ViewController (as in the following screenshot):

The CollectionView takes all the surface of the ViewController

Then create a new file of type "Cocoa Touch Class"

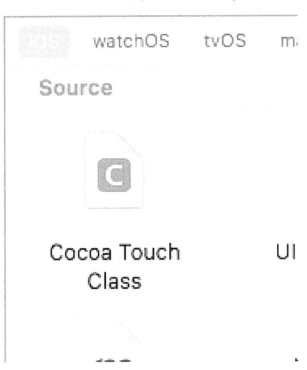

Choose a template for your n(

watchOS   tvOS   m.

Source

Cocoa Touch   UI
Class

The file must have as Subclass the type: "UICollectionViewCell", then validate:

Class:	CollectionViewCell
Subclass of:	UICollectionViewCell
	☐ Also create XIB file
Language:	Swift

Creating a UICollectionViewCell

Select the Cell inside the CollectionView and in the right pane of Xcode, select the third tab and assign it the class you just created:

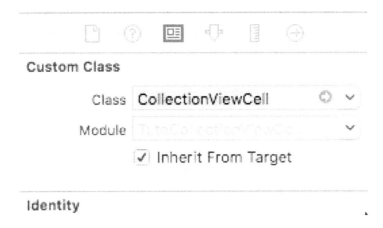

Then give an "Identifier" to the Cell (I call it "MyCell"):

Identify the cell

Add components to your cell (depending on what items you want to display). In this example we want to display a gallery of images so I chose to put in the cell a "UIImageView" and a "Label" So that each element will have an image and a title:

The representation of my cells

Now we are going to reference all the elements that make up our cell (for us it will be the UIImageView and the Label) and we reference them (or attach) to our class: "CollectionViewCell" that we created above. I name them: MyImage and MyLabel.

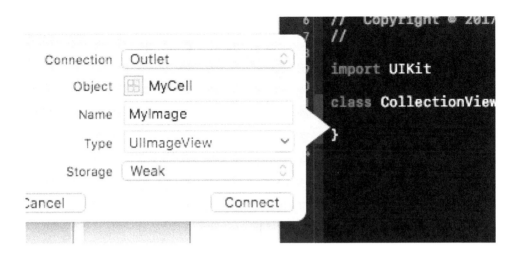

My two elements referenced on the following capture:

```
class CollectionViewCell: UICollectionViewCell {

    @IBOutlet weak var MyImage: UIImageView!
    @IBOutlet weak var MyLabel: UILabel!
}
```

Now reference the dataSource and the delegate of the CollectionView on the ViewController

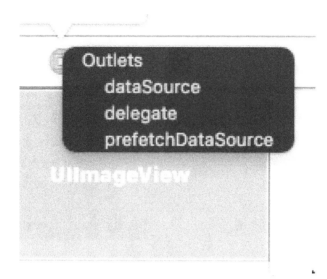

In your ViewController you must add the UICollectionViewDelegate and the UICollectionViewDataSource, as in the following screenshot:

The code

```
t
ontroller: UIViewController, UICollectionViewDelegate, UICollectionViewDataSource
```

We now create a table that contains all our titles and another that contains all our images. As I told you at the beginning of the chapter, I was not very original because my titles are named from Title 1 to Title 10 and for my images, I only have one that I used 10 time.

I know what you're saying. What is the point of creating a table if the value of the elements is 10 times the same? It's very simple, it's to show you the normal process, as if I had different images:

```
var TitresData: [String] = ["Titre 1", "Titre 2",
                            "Titre 3","Titre 4",
                            "Titre 5","Titre 6",
                            "Titre 7","Titre 8",
                            "Titre 9", "Titre 10"]

var ImagesData: [String] = ["moi.jpg", "moi.jpg",
                            "moi.jpg", "moi.jpg",
                            "moi.jpg", "moi.jpg",
                            "moi.jpg", "moi.jpg",
                            "moi.jpg", "moi.jpg"]
```

Our Arrays

We now have to create 3 functions for the Xcode error message to disappear (and also for it to work). Keep the name of the functions as on my screenshots. Here is the first, which is content to return the number of items in the collection.

```
func collectionView(_ collectionView: UICollectionView,
                    numberOfItemsInSection section: Int) -> Int {

    return TitresData.count;
}
```

The number of titles

The second is the most important because it is she who will allow us to manage the elements of each cell. As you can see on the next capture, I create a variable named "cell" of the same type as the class I created and assigned to the cell. Be careful, do not forget to fill in the correct identifier (here: MyCell) the one you have chosen for your cell.

The two most important lines are those that use the MyLabel and MyImage attributes (remember, that's how I named the Label for the title and the UIImageView for the image) so I'm indicating that the text of the label will be equal to the value of corresponding to its index in the table and the same for the image of the UIImageView.

To make it simpler: The first cell will have the first title of the title table and the first image of the image table, the second cell will be labeled the second element of the title table and the image will be the second of the table of titles. images, etc. (see next screenshot):

```
func collectionView(_ collectionView: UICollectionView,
                     cellForItemAt indexPath: IndexPath) -> UICollectionViewCell {

    var cell: CollectionViewCell = collectionView.dequeueReusableCell(
        withReuseIdentifier: "MyCell",
        for: indexPath) as! CollectionViewCell

    cell.MyLabel.text = TitresData[indexPath.row]
    cell.MyImage.image = UIImage(named: ImagesData[indexPath.row])
    return cell
}
```

The most important function

And lastly, the third and last one that just returns the current index:

```
func collectionView(_ collectionView: UICollectionView,
                    didSelectItemAt indexPath: IndexPath) {
    print("Cell \(indexPath.row)")
}
```

The last of the three necessary functions

Let's try it. Launch the application:

You should have a result almost identical to the following capture (except the photo):

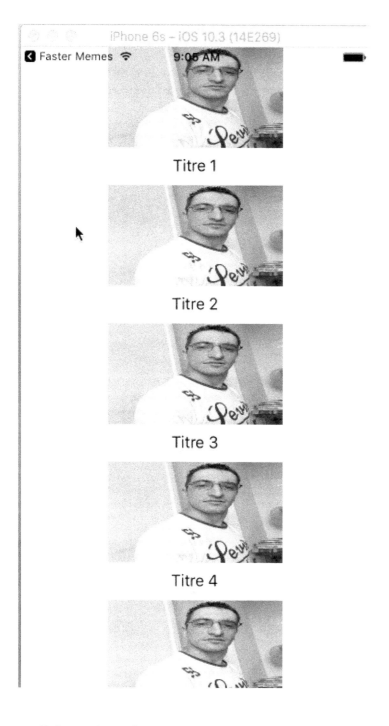

It all depends on the size and position of your base cell

By scrolling you will see the whole of your collection:

Ok, that's fine but let's see how to arrange our cells differently:

I will reduce the size of my cell and make it appear at the top left of my ViewController, as in the following screenshot:

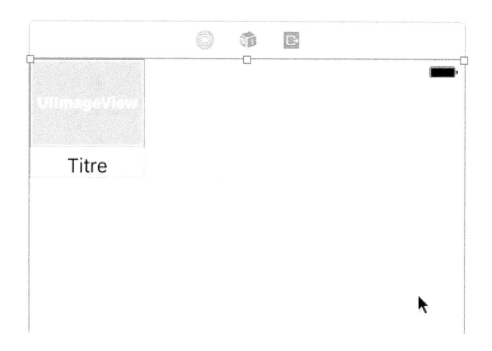

La Cellule

Let's try again:

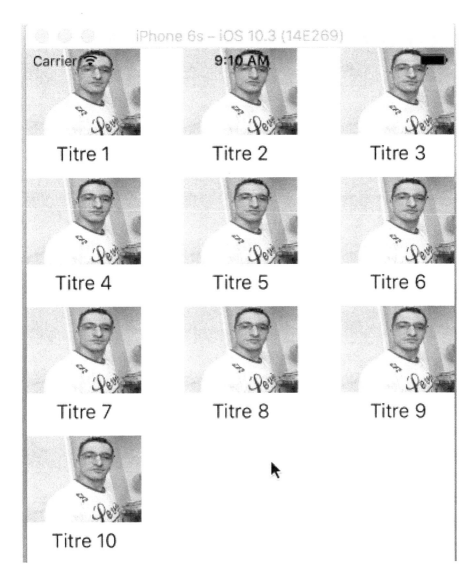

Let's try another way of doing things. Select your CollectionView and in the fourth tab of the right panel, select "Horizontal" in Scroll Direction:

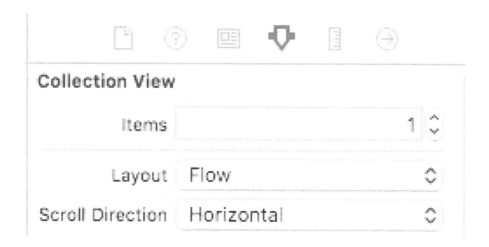

Changing the scroll direction

Now reduce the size of your CollectionView as I did on the next capture (I changed the background color of the CollectionView so you can see better but it will not be obvious on the capture):

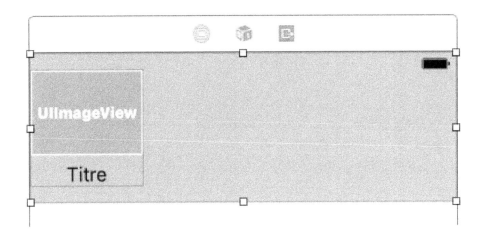

The CollectionView is shaped like a headband

Now the CollectionView should only display one item per line and scroll horizontally.

Let's try:

Items are displayed in "Horizontal"

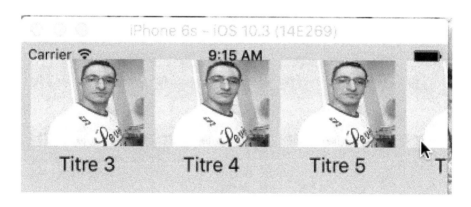

In bandeau

This chapter is now complete. We've learned how to manage data collections here so you can display your items in an orderly way, whether it's online or in a column and even in a grid.

Upcoming Chapter: The Layers.

Layers

In this chapter we will see the Layers and some manipulations concerning them. We start here with the CALayer class. Take a blank ViewController and put a UIImageView in the middle and then attach it to the Controller class:

Our UIImageView

```
@IBOutlet weak var ImageView: UIImageView!
override func viewDidLoad() {
    super.viewDidLoad()
```

It is referenced in the class of the ViewController

Now we are going to create a variable that will represent the Layer of our UIImageView, doing like this:

```
var lay: CALayer {
    return ImageView.layer
}
```

The variable lay represents the Layer of our UIImageView

Then we create a function or we will change some properties of the Layer, then this function will be launched in the ViewDidLoad:

```
override func viewDidLoad() {
    super.viewDidLoad()


    settingLayer()

}
func settingLayer() {
    lay.backgroundColor = UIColor.gray.cgColor
    lay.borderWidth = 5.0
    lay.borderColor = UIColor.black.cgColor
    lay.shadowOpacity = 0.6
    lay.shadowRadius = 15.0
}
```

We are changing some properties of our UIImageView

We have changed (in order):
  The background color (in gray), the thickness of the border (5), the color of the border (in black), the opacity of the shadow (0.6 or 60%) and the radius of the shadow (15).

So we should have a UIImageView that is gray in color (as long as it does not contain any image of course) with a 5-point thick black border with a radius shadow 15 that has an opacity of 60 percent.

Let's try to see what it gives (capture to the next image):

Carrier 🛜   7:19 AM

Our UIImageView after changing some properties of its Layer

I will now show you how to round up your photos perfectly (as do more and more sites and applications). For this example I will take a square image but has a rounded outline, so we will see the result.

Here is the image in question (which I already loaded in our UIImageView):

Our example image

I give you the function with the properties of our Layer, adding at the end the property that will allow us to round our image. This is the property: "cornerRadius". You will see that for the roundness to be excellent we must give it as value: half the width of our image (the image must be square):

```
func settingLayer() {
    lay.backgroundColor = UIColor.gray.cgColor
    lay.borderWidth = 5.0
    lay.borderColor = UIColor.black.cgColor
    lay.shadowOpacity = 0.6
    lay.shadowRadius = 15.0
    lay.cornerRadius = ImageView.frame.width / 2
}
```

With the cornerRadius

I get the width of our UIImageView in its "frame" property and I divide by two. Let's do a test (next capture) and then we'll attack with another type of Layers.

The result of our Image

What's great is that the rendering immediately adapted the border and shadow properties on our new image.

The GradientLayer or CAGradientLayer is the Layer that will allow us to manage color gradients. In this paragraph, as an example, we will create a "Power Gauge" style gradient from Red to Green.

To do this insert a View in your ViewController (the one in the previous paragraph will do the trick), then reference it in the class. I show you the View that I created (I tinted it on the capture so you can recognize it):

My View for the gradient

We call our View: ViewForGradient:

```
@IBOutlet weak var ImageView: UIImageView!
@IBOutlet weak var ViewForGradient: UIView!
```

My View is now attached to the class

I decided to put the code of the gradient in a function for more clarity (it will of course not forget to call the function when launching the View.In this function I create an instance of the class CAGradientLayer I stores in the gradientLayer variable, as you see on the following snapshot:

```
func SetGradient(){
    let gradientLayer = CAGradientLayer()
    gradientLayer.frame = ViewForGradient.bounds
    gradientLayer.colors = [

        cgColorGradient(red: 209.0, green: 0.0, blue: 0.0),
        cgColorGradient(red: 255.0, green: 102.0, blue: 0.0),
        cgColorGradient(red: 140.0, green: 170.0, blue: 0.0),
        cgColorGradient(red: 0.0, green: 240.0, blue: 0.0)
                           ]

    gradientLayer.startPoint = CGPoint(x: 0, y: 0)
    gradientLayer.endPoint = CGPoint(x: 1, y: 0)
    ViewForGradient.layer.addSublayer(gradientLayer)
}
```

The function that will handle the gradient

65

Below the instantiation I tell him that the frame of our gradient corresponds to the bounds of the View we created. Then I have to inform him a table which contains the colors of my gradient.

The choice of colors and the number that your gradient will contain you belongs to you. But before going any further, let me tell you that this array of colors expects CGColor type values and if you see that this array is composed of several elements named cgColorGradient it's because it's just a function that I created to convert the colors to the correct format.

By the way here is the function, then I will come back to the main code:

```
func cgColorGradient(
    red: CGFloat,
    green: CGFloat,
    blue: CGFloat) -> AnyObject {

    return UIColor(
        red: red/255.0,
        green: green/255.0,
        blue: blue/255.0,
        alpha: 1.0).cgColor as AnyObject
}
```

I convert the colors to the correct format

Nothing really complicated here, let's go back to the previous code if you want it.

After our color table we have the startPoint and endPoint attributes that correspond respectively to the beginning and the end of the gradient in your View.
But you have to know that the values here go from 0 to 1, knowing that for X, 0 is equivalent on the left and 1 is equivalent on the right. As for Y, 0 corresponds to the High and 1, corresponds to the Low.

Finally, let's just say that the Layer of our View is equal to our gradientLayer thanks to the addSublayer method.

And do not forget to call our function that creates the gradient in the ViewDidLoad:

```
override func viewDidLoad() {
    super.viewDidLoad()


    settingLayer()
    SetGradient()

}
```

We call our function

We will do a test (on the next capture) and then we will move to another type of Layer. As you see (at home, because the capture is less visible) it's quite powerful. You can add colors or change the position, shape etc.

Carrier 📶   8:56 AM

Our Gradient

The CAReplicatorLayer is a type of Layer that allows you to duplicate a Layer a number of times, to create cool effects. To begin, insert a View into your ViewController (just insert it below the gradient of the previous paragraph) and then reference it in the class.

In this example we will create a circular and animated loading effect that looks like this:

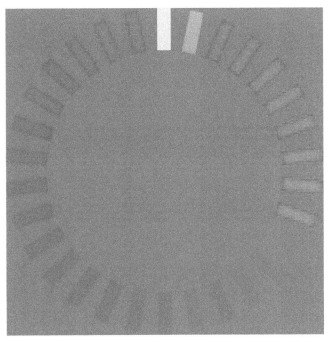

Difficult to represent an animation in a book

Our View

We refer to it as: ViewForReplicator:

70

```
@IBOutlet weak var ViewForReplicator: UIView!
```

Now, let's create a function that will contain all the code that will handle the Layer. The function contains a lot of line so I split the code into blocks that are spread over several captures in a row.

```
func SetReplicator(){

    // 1
    let replicatorLayer = CAReplicatorLayer()
    replicatorLayer.frame = ViewForReplicator.bounds

    // 2
    let nbInstances = 30
    replicatorLayer.instanceCount = nbInstances
    replicatorLayer.instanceDelay = CFTimeInterval(1 / Float(nbInstances))
    replicatorLayer.preservesDepth = false
    replicatorLayer.instanceColor = UIColor.white.cgColor
```

The first two blocks of our function

In block 1, we create an instance of the class CAReplicatorLayer and we name our object: replicatorLayer. Then as usual we have to fill the frame of our Layer within the limits of our View.

In block 2, we create a variable that contains the number 30 that will correspond to the number of instances of our animation. Then we tell him how long each instance lasts and the color of the original instance:

71

```
// 3
replicatorLayer.instanceRedOffset = 0.0
replicatorLayer.instanceGreenOffset = -0.5
replicatorLayer.instanceBlueOffset = -0.5
replicatorLayer.instanceAlphaOffset = 0.0
```

The offset of each color channel

This block 3 represents the offset of each channel of the instance color. If you do not understand at the moment, it will come when you have seen the result. Let's go on :

```
// 4
let angle = Float(M_PI * 2.0) / Float(nbInstances)
replicatorLayer.instanceTransform = CATransform3DMakeRotation(
    CGFloat(angle), 0.0, 0.0, 1.0)

ViewForReplicator.layer.addSublayer(replicatorLayer)

// 5
let instanceLayer = CALayer()
let layerWidth: CGFloat = 10.0
let midX = ViewForReplicator.bounds.midX - layerWidth / 2.0
instanceLayer.frame = CGRect(
    x: midX,
    y: 0.0,
    width: layerWidth,
    height: layerWidth * 3.0)

instanceLayer.backgroundColor = UIColor.white.cgColor
replicatorLayer.addSublayer(instanceLayer)
```

Blocks 4 and 5 of the function

In block 4, we manage the angle of each animation slide with rotation. In block 5, we create an instance of a Layer for each slat by populating parameters such as its size and position. I do not need to explain the addSubLayer method anymore. We have seen it above.

72

```
// 6
let fadeAnimation = CABasicAnimation(keyPath: "opacity")
fadeAnimation.fromValue = 1.0
fadeAnimation.toValue = 0.0
fadeAnimation.duration = 1
fadeAnimation.repeatCount = Float(Int.max)

// 7
instanceLayer.opacity = 0.0
instanceLayer.add(fadeAnimation, forKey: "FadeAnimation")
}
```

Blocks 6 and 7 are there only to manage the fade of the animation

And finally, do not forget to call the function in the ViewDidLoad for which starts at startup:

```
override func viewDidLoad() {
    super.viewDidLoad()


    settingLayer()
    SetGradient()
    SetReplicator()
}
```

We launch the function

Sorry for the result that will only be partial since you will not see the animation on my capture:

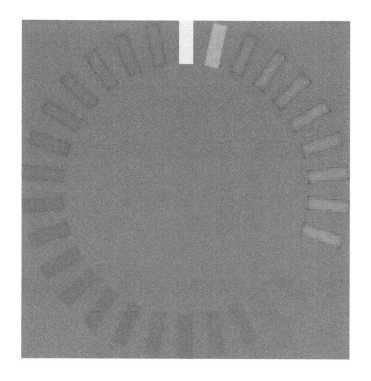

Our animation

There are of course others, but we will not be able to see them all. I will still tell you a minimum because some of them may be useful.

The CAScrollLayer

The CAScrollLayer allows you to manage Scrolling in a Layer, but unfortunately it is very basic so I have not reserved a paragraph.

The CATextLayer

The CATextLayer provides a quick but easy way to manage text, such as font size, alignment, and other text-related properties.

The CATiledLayer

CATiledLayer allows you to create Tiles images. I have never tried it.

The CAEmitterLayer

The CAEmitterLayer is the one in this list that would have deserved a paragraph or even a chapter because it allows you to create animated particle effects. He is nice enough when you need this kind of effects.

Here is this chapter is now over, in the next we will talk about this powerful and practical feature that is called "Extension" and that allows to change the behavior of classes even when we do not have access to the source code .

Extensions

As I told you briefly in the previous chapter, the extension is a very useful and very powerful feature of the Swift language as it allows you to modify the behavior of classes for which you do not even have access to the source code.

Imagine that you need to add methods to the Double class. You will tell me, yes, but for what purpose I will add methods to this class?

Let me give you an example:
You create a Double variable that you name "meters" (which represents the meters), you will use the Doubles in your application, almost for the sole purpose of converting distances and you would like that every time you take a number (of type Double) to have the right to make a point just after your number (or variable) to call a method on that number.

For example, the Cm method that each time you use it on a number (which is assumed to be meters) returns its value in Centimeters.

This is possible with extensions and of course we can do much more interesting things, but I can not reveal everything in the introduction.

In my case, I usually create a separate file that includes all my Extensions, but you can add them at the bottom or top of any class. It's just a matter of organization.

For this example I created a Swift file that I named: "MyExtensions" and I'm starting to create an Extension for the Double class. To create an Extension, it's very simple just do it like this:

```
extension Double {

}
```

Extension of type Double

We will create an attribute "cm" that will return us the equivalent of the current number in centimeters (assuming that in our code our number is in meters:

```
extension Double {

    var cm:Double {
        return self * 100.0
    }

}
```

Our first extension

Go in your code and after typing a double, put a point just after as if you wanted to call a method on this double. You see that the word "cm" is proposed to you. Choose it and display all this in a print as on my capture:

```
override func viewDidLoad() {
    super.viewDidLoad()

    settingLayer()
    SetGradient()
    SetReplicator()

    print(5.00.cm)
}
```

I request conversion from 5 to centimeters

Result :

Let's create more conversions for our Extension:

```
extension Double {

    var cm:Double {
        return self * 100.0
    }
    var km: Double {
        return self * 1_000.0
    }

    var m: Double {
        return self
    }

    var mm: Double {
        return self / 1_000.0
    }

    var ft: Double {
        return self / 3.28084
    }

}
```

Extension Double

We have created the units km / m (which is the basic unit, but you can change) / mm / and also ft (foot in English).

Now every time you put a point after a Double, you can convert it to the unit of your choice.

Let's create an Extension on the Int type but with an interesting example:

```swift
extension Int {
    func boucles(task: () -> Void) {
        for _ in 0..<self {
            task()
        }
    }
}
```

In this code I create a method loops and I tell him that it will have to run the number of times corresponding to the number on which I use it and that it will have to execute the code that I will give it. Ok I'm aware that it's not clear said like that, but let's see a more telling example:

```swift
5.boucles {
    print("Hello")
}
```

I choose the number 5 (an Int) and when I put a point after, I have the possibility to use the loops method that I just created and this method I can give it code between braces and in this code I give it request to show me a print.

Result:

```
Hello
Hello
Hello
Hello
Hello
```

You see, the "loops" method executes the code I give it in braces the number of times I mentioned in the Int that uses the method.

View

Now let's take a look at the Views to create an Extension for the UIImageView type.

But be careful to create Extensions on the Views you have to import UIKit into your Extensions file. Our Extension will allow us to use a method that will round the Images:

```
extension UIImageView {

    func Rond() -> UIImageView{
        self.layer.cornerRadius = self.frame.Width/2
        self.clipsToBounds = true
        return self
    }
}
```

Extension for the type UIImageView

Do you remember the chapter on Collections? Return to the function that assigns Images to each cell and add the next to last line of the following capture:

```
cell.MyLabel.text = TitresData[indexPath.row]
    cell.MyImage.image = UIImage(named: ImagesData[inde
    cell.MyImage.Rond()
    return cell
```

Result :

Rounded images

I warned you that if the View was not square the rounding was not great by halving the width.

This chapter is now complete. As you have seen, Extensions are a pretty powerful mechanism of Swift language.

Of course you can go further by using them, but this book goes to the basics after you understand the principle, you will use them according to your needs.

In the next chapter (which also did not deserve to be in chapter form but rather in paragraph because of its size) we will see how to convert a View into UIImage.

Convert a View into UIImage

So here we'll see how to convert a View to UIImage and even how to save a View to the device gallery. We start by creating an extension of the type UIView and we add the function of the following capture:

```swift
extension UIView {

    func createImage() -> UIImage {
        var rect: CGRect = self.frame

        UIGraphicsBeginImageContext(rect.size)
        let context: CGContext = UIGraphicsGetCurrentContext()!
        self.layer.render(in: context)
        let img = UIGraphicsGetImageFromCurrentImageContext()
        UIGraphicsEndImageContext()

        return img!
    }

}
```

Code to convert a View into UIImage

To do this we need to manipulate the Contexts, but they will not be detailed in this book. Now, since all components are Views, you can convert any of them to UIImage.

For this you just have to put a point after the View that you want to convert to UIImage and select the function createImage

For example, in my iPhone application "Faster Memes" the user can create memes with four images, as if he was telling a story in the same. There are four UIImageViews in the main ViewController, each containing a text strip on a black background underneath.

So I need not to save an Image but the four at the same time in the form of a single image (and with their text and more), so here the principle of converting a View UIImage is very convenient. Here is a template of my View that needs to be converted:

The View model that I convert to UIImage in Faster Memes

That's it, you understand that with this conversion system, saving this kind of View is very useful. But let's go back to our code. We will now create a function in this Extension that will directly save the View in the device gallery.

It's very simple, we take the code and instead of returning the image we save it with the function

"UIImageWriteToSavedPhotosAlbum", giving him as an argument our image to save. As on the following capture:

```
func saveViewAsImage() -> Void {
    var rect: CGRect = self.frame

    UIGraphicsBeginImageContext(rect.size)
    let context: CGContext = UIGraphicsGetCurrentContext()!
    self.layer.render(in: context)
    let img = UIGraphicsGetImageFromCurrentImageContext()
    UIGraphicsEndImageContext()

    UIImageWriteToSavedPhotosAlbum(img!, nil, nil, nil)

}
```

The same as the previous one with one exception

Do not forget to set the return type to "Void".

Before doing a test, we must think about asking permission to use the camera to the user, (in the file: info.plist) otherwise it will not work. Here is the line to add:

Privacy - Photo Library Usage Des... ◇   String $(PRODUCT_NAME) a besoin d'utiliser les photos

The phrase cut to the left is:
Privacy - Photo Library Usage Description

On the right, put what you want.

I put the following code in the ViewDidLoad function:

```
self.view.saveViewAsImage()
```

We save the View

And the image will be saved when the controller is launched. Let's try:

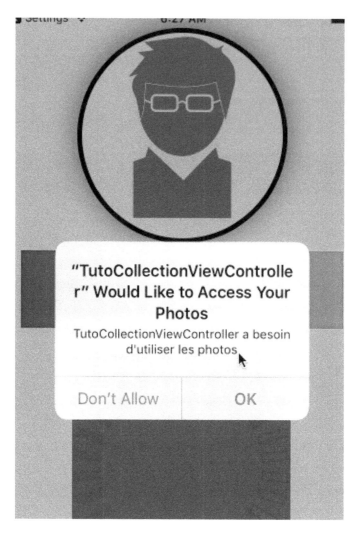

The application requests permission to use the Photos gallery

I validate, the application runs normally and if I go to my photo gallery, I find my View which has been saved as an image (next capture).
Voilà ce chapitre est terminé, nous pouvons attaquer le ScrollView pour pouvoir faire défiler une View sur l'écran.

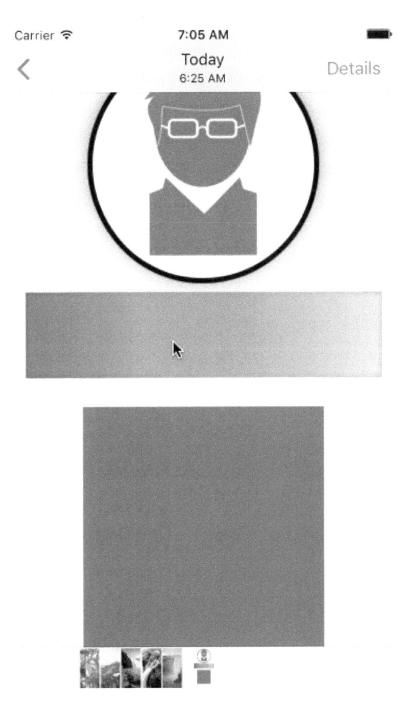

The View is an image and in our gallery

ScrollView

We are attacking a Scroll system to be able to scroll an image that is much larger than the screen. Let's start by inserting a ScrollView in our controller by making it take all the width and height of the controller.

I said that you will not see it in the code, that my Image is already assigned to my UIImageView and that it is much larger than the screen. Here is the picture I used:

Then, at the bottom of the window in Xcode, clicking on the triangle, assign him the "Reset to Suggested Constraints". Then reference your ScrollView in the controller class:

```
@IBOutlet weak var ImageView: UIImageView!
@IBOutlet weak var ScrollView: UIScrollView!
```

We refer to our ScrollView

And in the ViewDidLoad here is the code:

```
override func viewDidLoad() {
    super.viewDidLoad()

    // Do any additional setup after loading the view.

    ImageView.sizeToFit()
    ScrollView.addSubview(ImageView)
    ScrollView.contentSize = ImageView.frame.size
}
```

ScrollView settings

You have to use the sizeToFit method on your UIImageView, then we have to add our UIImageView as under our ScrollView (this is the penultimate line of the capture).

To finish and it is important to understand it: it is necessary to signify that the size of the ScrollView is equal to the size of our UIImageView (or you can choose the zone if you want to be able to scroll only on a part of the 'picture). We do this with the contentSize method of our ScrollView. If you forget it, it will not work.

All right, it was pretty simple at the moment. We will try to see what this gives. Of course the scrolling tests on a book are not obvious to show, but you can always do the test at home. Let's launch the application.

As you can see on the next capture, the image is very large and with the ScrollView, you can move anywhere in the image.

In the next paragraph, we will set up the Zoom on the ScrollView and we will be able to set the Minimum Zoom and the Maximum Zoom.

To set up the Zoom, you must link the delegate of your ScrollView to your controller. The easiest way to do this is to do it in the Designer with a right click.

Then in the controller class you have to add this line:

```
UIViewController, UIScrollViewDelegate
```

The delegate of the ScrollView

Then in the ViewDidLoad you have to add some lines of code that I will detail you. I put you the complete function:

```
override func viewDidLoad() {
    super.viewDidLoad()

    // Do any additional setup after loading the view.
    ScrollView.delegate = self
    ImageView.sizeToFit()
    ScrollView.addSubview(ImageView)
    ScrollView.contentSize = ImageView.frame.size
    ScrollView.minimumZoomScale = 0.05
    ScrollView.maximumZoomScale = 1.0
}
```

Our ViewDidLoad with Zoom Settings

The first line links the delegate of the ScrollView to the current controller, then the last two set the minimum and maximum Zoom, knowing that a Zoom of 1.0 corresponds to the actual size of the image, so you understand that 0.05 corresponds to 5 % of its size.

Of course I could have put a maximum zoom of 3.0, which would correspond to three times its actual size, but I find that on the contrary, the interest in this example is to reduce the image and not to enlarge.

You must add a function of the delegate to tell it to return the UIImageView. This function is here (do not change its name):

```
func viewForZooming(in scrollView: UIScrollView) -> UIView? {
    return ImageView
}
```

The function of the delegate

Let's try it:

With Zoom to a minimum

With the zoom at least that's what it gives you see that it is very responsive by zooming out with the touch. We can of course zoom in if we want to enlarge our image, doing the manipulation in the other direction. I put a capture of a size visible in its entirety on the screen of my device.

This chapter is now complete. In the next we will talk about Alerts.

Alert

We will start with simple windows, which are the equivalent of computer dialogs. Let's attack the code directly:

```
func CreerAlerte(titleTexte : String, messageText : String) {
    let alert = UIAlertController(title: titleTexte,message:messageText,
                            preferredStyle : UIAlertControllerStyle.alert)

    let TexteAction = UIAlertAction(
        title: "Ok",
        style: .default,
        handler:{ action in self.Ok()})

    let CancelAction = UIAlertAction(
        title: "Retour",
        style: .cancel,
        handler: nil)

    alert.addAction(TexteAction)

    alert.addAction(CancelAction) // Cancel

    self.present(alert, animated: true, completion: nil)
}
```

I am grouping the alert code into a function

I create a function that will automatically assign the title and message of my alert. I start by creating an AlertController by giving it the title and the message I will send to the function. I mention that the type of alert will be "alert", (there are other types).

Then I create two UIAlertAction (these are the buttons). I give them a title, a style and for the first you will notice that I give it a function as action. That is, a function that will execute if the user taps on this button.

I add my two actions to my "alert". And I do a self.present, giving my "alert" as an argument. Which means that I launch the alert here.

```
func Ok() {
    //Mettez ce que vous voulez ICI
}
```

Here is the function that executes when you type the first button of the alert (As you see, as far as I'm concerned, I did not put anything for this example but you are free to add code) .

```
override func viewDidAppear(_ animated: Bool) {
    self.CreerAlerte(
        titleTexte : "Mon super titre",
        messageText : "Message de mon alerte")
}
```

Then, very important I parameter the function that creates and launches the alert, not in the ViewDidLoad, but in the viewDidAppear (it will write yourself).

We make a test, by launching the application:

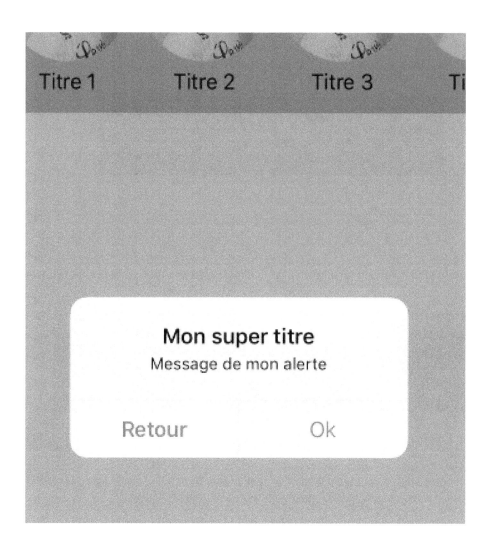

The result when launching the application

ActionSheet alerts are menu alerts that are found on IPhones when you tap the + button (usually at the top right). They do not launch into a ViewDidLoad, but in support of a button.

To create an ActionSheet Alert (which starts at the touch of a button) you have to replace the alert style with ActionSheet like this:

```
var alert = UIAlertController(
    title: "Menu",
    message:"",
    preferredStyle : UIAlertControllerStyle.actionSheet)
```

An ActionSheet alert

And before doing the present, we must add:

```
alert.modalPresentationStyle = .popover
```

Style of presentation: Popover

I added some buttons before showing you the result, so that it is more speaking (see next screenshot).

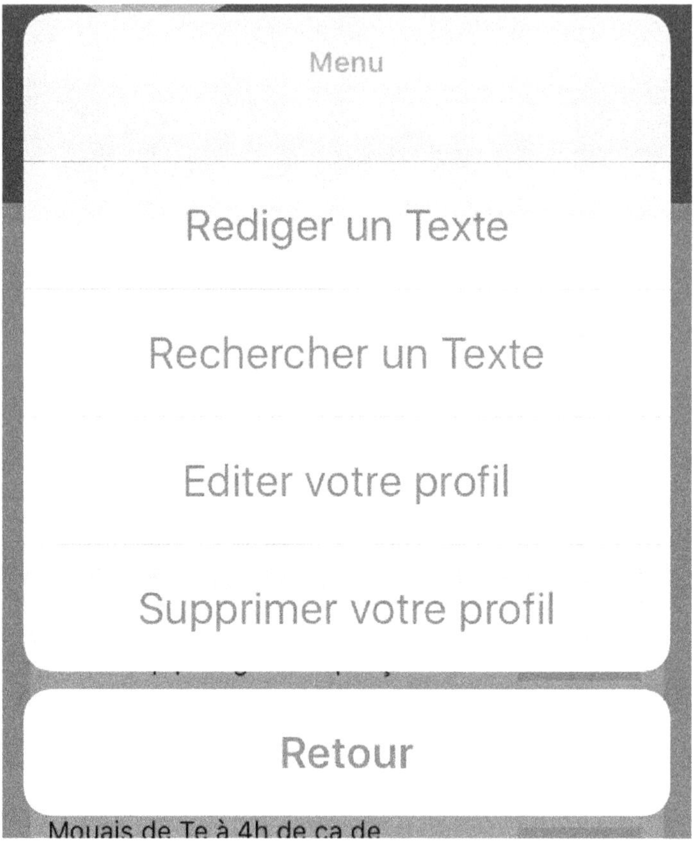

This chapter is now complete.

Conclusions

Here we come to the end of this short book. I hope it has been helpful to you. Let's review what we have learned.

We learned to post on Facebook and Twitter social networks and with images. We also know how to recover images from the camera gallery.

Then we saw the collections to display elements as we wish. All you need is a collection of items to display and you have seen that you do not have to enter the items one by one.

Then we learned some very practical things about Layers, which allows us now to manage the styles of our components but also to make gradients or animated effects rather nice.

Then one of my favorite features: Extensions, which happens to be a way to modify the code that we do not have access, to improve or add functions.

We have seen a (short) chapter on how to convert a View into UIImage which you will surely be very useful in specific scenarios but one thing is sure. I looked for a moment before finding this solution for one of my projects and it was certainly not in French.

You now know how to use a ScrollView in a simple way. I do not know about you, but me at first, the ScrollView in my projects was something chaotic and I did not handle it well at all.

There I explained you in a simple and clear way and you even know how to use Zoom.

The alerts, these modal boxes (or menus), I'm sure that now it seems much easier to set up, is not it?

If you bought this book on Amazon, I will ask you to take a minute to give it a note and commentary to: not only direct readers who might buy it but also help me promote it.

It is thanks to that that I managed to leave the consequences of my previous books by teaching the readers always more and more tricks.

If you wish you can follow me on Twitter: @JulienFAUJANET, or if you have a question you can send me an email to: julienfaujanet@gmail.com. I will be happy to answer you.

...Thank you...

Bibliography

Manuel indispensable pour Unity :

Dans ce livre vous apprendrez de façon claire et précise comment créer des jeux vidéos avec le moteur de jeux : Unity. Même si vous n'avez aucune notion de programmation, elles vous seront apprises de façon simple. L'auteur à sorti plusieurs jeux Smartphones grâce à ce moteur de jeux et sur différentes plateformes : Windows Phone / Android / IOS. Mais vous pouvez aussi créer vos jeux pour d'autres supports : Linux / Apple TV etc....

L'adultère, les ex, les virus, comment les démasquer :

Dans ce livre vous allez apprendre les bases pour démasquer un adultère ou un conjoint menteur d'un point de vue informatique ou tout simplement comment vous cacher d'une personne un peu trop curieuse.

Bien commencer avec Python 3 :

Dans ce livre vous apprendrez les bases du langage de programmation Python dans sa version 3. Si vous voulez apprendre les bases (ainsi que quelques astuces) ce livre est celui qu'il vous faut. Vous apprendrez ce qu'il faut savoir de façon claire et rapide.

Python 3, niveau intermédiaire :

Dans ce livre vous passerez au niveau supérieur si vous avez les bases en Python, vous apprendrez comment créer des logiciels de manipulations d'images avec Tkinter et la librairie Pil (Pillow)

Python 3, niveau avancé :

Dans ce livre, vous monterez encore d'un cran et le thème principal du livre est d'apprendre à dissimuler des données dans une image (ce domaine se nomme : sténographie). Ne faîtes pas l'erreur de croire que c'est quelque chose de compliqué... Pas avec ce livre.

Python 3, de débutant à avancé :

Ce livre est le regroupement des trois précédents livres en un seul volume. Mais cela fait de lui un des livres les plus achetés sur le langage Python. Trois livres pour le prix d'un, c'est le livre qu'il vous faut.

Bien commencer avec Pygame :

Vous voulez créer des jeux vidéos simples avec le langage de programmation Python, mais vous ne voulez pas apprendre une technologie compliqué et vous souhaitez que votre apprentissage soit assez rapide ? Ce livre vous apportera les bases qu'il vous faut.

Automatisation avec Python :

Vous voulez apprendre comment faire exécuter des taches à votre ordinateur grâce au langage de programmation Python ? Vous voulez créer un système qui clique automatiquement ou qui se connecte à un site ? Vous voulez créer un « bot » ? Vous êtes devant le bon livre.

Créez des logiciels facilement avec Visual Studio :

Vous voulez apprendre à créer des logiciels Windows de la façon la plus simple et la plus rapide possible ? C'est le bon livre. Vous pensez que quand vous lisez un livre c'est toujours plus dur que ce que vous avait annoncé le titre ? Sachez que ce livre est à la porté d'un enfant de 11 / 12 ans. Si vous pensez toujours que ce livre peut être compliqué : Pensez-vous que ce soit compliqué de sélectionner des éléments dans une colonne pour les faire glisser avec la souris là ou vous voulez qu'ils apparaissent dans votre logiciel ? Parce que c'est comme ça que vous allez créer votre premier logiciel.

Les Contrôles Windows Form :

Ce livre regroupe des astuces et explications pour le livre précédent. Si vous débutez avec la création en Visual studio, ce livre vous sera très utile. En fait ce livre n'est qu'un (gros) plus pour les débutants et intermédiaires. Il explique comment utiliser certains éléments et fait gagner beaucoup de temps au lecteur.

L' API Twitter en Python tome 1 :

Ce livre vous permettra de manipuler Twitter en Python.
Pour automatiser toutes les taches que vous désirez
comme : écrire des tweets, retweeter automatiquement,
faire des recherches d'utilisateurs. Vous voulez un « bot »
pour Twitter ? Lisez ce livre.

www.ingramcontent.com/pod-product-compliance
Lightning Source LLC
LaVergne TN
LVHW052304060326
832902LV00021B/3694